# Apes Monkeys

LEVEL **2** READER

READING LEVEL 2 GRADES 1 TO 3

Written by Kathryn Knight
Art Copyright © Edizioni Larus S.p.A.

The DALMATIAN PRESS name is a trademark of Dalmatian Publishing Group,
Franklin, Tennessee 37068-2068. 1-866-418-2572.

DalmatianPress23401010958F16842264-03/11

# Gorilla

Gorillas of Africa are the biggest apes. They have stout bodies with long arms, which they use to "knuckle walk." Gorillas are *herbivores* (plant eaters), munching on stems, twigs, and leaves. They live in small groups led by the males, called silverbacks. Leaders protect their families by pretending to attack. They stand up, rip up bushes, yell, and pound their chests.

Baby gorillas are cuddled by all the
females, but they
sleep next to their
mothers. When the
mother wakes
up, the baby
jumps on her
back and
rides along.

Young gorillas like to wrestle, slide down
grassy banks, and climb trees. The big gorillas
sleep on the ground. Youngsters and females
snooze in the trees.

# Chimpanzee

Chimpanzees are clever apes and can use simple tools. They live in African forests in tribes. A male—not the strongest, but the most expert—leads each group.

Chimpanzees spend most of their time caring for young, grooming, and looking for fruits, leaves, and insects to eat. When it gets dark, they scamper up trees to sleep.

Mothers keep their babies close for three
years. When the mother moves, her baby
hangs on to her furry lap. Later, little chimps
ride "piggyback." When they're big enough,
they walk beside their mothers.

A baby chimpanzee
may suck its thumb,
just like a little girl
or boy.

# Guenon

Guenon (guh-**nawns**) are African monkeys that live in groups of about forty. They have tough skin on their bottoms and can sit on tree branches where it is safe. The mothers cling to their babies as they swing through the trees.

**Vervet guenons** eat insects, lizards, and fruits. They scream out an alarm if a leopard, eagle, or snake is nearby.

The **putty-nose guenon** of the forest is very gentle.

**De Brazza's guenons** live along riverbanks and eat tropical lizards called geckoes.

The **dwarf guenon** is the smallest African monkey. It lives in swampy forests.

**Mustached guenons** like thick forests. They hang out in high trees and only eat fruit.

# Mandrill

Mandrills look like apes, but they are actually the largest monkeys. Their bright face colors are quite remarkable. Mandrills live on the edge of forests. They spend most of their time looking for roots, fruits, plants, insects, worms, frogs, and lizards to eat. They "talk" to each other with grunts and cries.

Mandrills live
in tribes with
a male leader.
He defends them
from enemies like
leopards, large
snakes, and eagles.
When a male mandrill sees an enemy, his face,
chest, and hands become even brighter. He

flings out his
arms, tips back
his head, and
opens his mouth
to show long,
sharp teeth.
Even leopards
get scared!

# Colobus Monkey

The colobus (**call**-uh-bus) is one of the most beautiful monkeys in Africa. A newborn colobus is all white. Then its fur changes over time to a soft black with white trim. The colobus lives in the treetops. It is shy and gentle. It scurries away from branch to branch at the first hint of danger.

# Baboon

The baboon is a big monkey that lives in large tribes in the African grasslands. A baboon walks on all fours on the palms and soles of its feet. Every day these monkeys may walk three miles looking for grasses, fruits, insects, and small animals to eat. They take time to groom each other, which makes friendships stronger.

# Orangutan

Orangutans of Asia are the world's largest tree-dwelling animals. These apes use their long, strong arms to swing from one tree to another without touching the ground. Their name means "man of the forest."

An orangutan's face shows feelings, such as fear, happiness, and sadness.

Orangutans are very clever. They use big leaves as umbrellas when it rains!

Orangutans don't live in tribes. They like to live alone in the rainforest. They eat fruits, leaves, small animals, and eggs. Mothers have only one baby at a time. They look after each baby for six or seven years.

# Gibbon

Gibbons are lively apes. They have round heads and flat faces that look almost human. And they walk upright on two legs. Gibbons have long arms and they swing easily through the trees. A gibbon's arms are so long, they touch the ground when the gibbon is standing up straight. Like all other apes, gibbons do not have tails.

The siamang (**see**-uh-mang) is a large gibbon, about 3 feet tall with black fur. It has a sack of stretchy skin on its throat. This sack helps it make loud cries that can be heard miles away.

# Proboscis Monkey

The proboscis (pro-**boss**-kiss) monkey gets its name from the male's big nose. (Proboscis means snout or nose.) The large nose helps make the monkey's screams even louder. Females are smaller than males, but both have tails as long as their bodies.

These friendly Asian monkeys live along the coast or near riverbanks. They eat leaves, fruit, and flowers. They spend most of their time in trees, but they are also great swimmers. Some have been seen swimming in the sea, far, far away from the coast.

# Langur

Langurs (lawn-**goors**) are also
called leaf monkeys because they eat so many
leaves. They have long, slender hands and feet
and long tails.

**Hanuman langurs** are the most common
monkeys in India. They are excellent climbers
and jumpers. They often live close to humans
and hang out around old temples. Indians even
train them for street shows!

Each kind of langur has its own look. The **spectacled langur** has pale skin around its eyes. It looks like it is wearing spectacles (glasses).

The **white-bearded langur** has thick white fur on its cheeks. It is quick! It can run 20 miles an hour.

The **douc langur** lives in the rainforest. It can live for thirty years, but there are very few left in the wild.

# Golden Snub-nosed Monkey

This rare monkey has a lovely thick, soft coat of golden red. It gets its name from its short, stumpy nose. It lives in trees and can be found in bamboo forests of China, as far up as snowfields on the mountains. Local people call this animal the "snow monkey."

# Howler Monkey

The howler is the biggest monkey of the Americas. It can weigh up to twenty pounds. This monkey screams, or howls, to say "This is my land!" The screams are so loud, they can be heard as far as three miles away! The howler monkey likes to stay in trees, moving from branch to branch.

# Spider Monkey

Spider monkeys of South America have long, thin arms and legs. They are great gymnasts in the branches. They can zip from branch to branch and jump as far as forty feet. Their long tails work like hooks and are very useful for picking fruit.

# Tamarin

The tamarin is a small monkey. It has a mane of white around its face. When a male fights, his mane stands up to make him look stronger and taller.

# Squirrel Monkey

Cute little squirrel monkeys live in tribes in the treetops. As they jump, they use their long tails for balance. They crack walnuts and eggs by smashing them against branches.

## Owl Monkey

Owl monkeys are the only *nocturnal* (active at night) monkeys. They live in small family groups.

During the day, the family sleeps side-by-side in hollow trees.

## Woolly Monkey

The woolly monkey sleeps high up on a branch. It wraps its long tail around its body *and* the branch so it won't fall off.

Good night, monkeys.